THE
Passionate Sailor

NAT PHILBRICK

ILLUSTRATIONS BY
GARY PATTERSON

A FULL CIRCLE BOOK

CONTEMPORARY
BOOKS, INC.
CHICAGO ▪ NEW YORK

Published by Contemporary Books, Inc.
180 North Michigan Avenue, Chicago, Illinois 60601
Manufactured in the United States of America
International Standard Book Number: 0-8092-5018-7

Published simultaneously in Canada by Beaverbooks, Ltd.
195 Allstate Parkway, Valleywood Business Park
Markham, Ontario L3R 4T8 Canada

BOAT LOVER

To my parents, Marianne and Tom Philbrick—two sailors who taught me that nothing is worth doing unless it's done passionately.

                                        Nat Philbrick

It's with great admiration that I dedicate
this book to the insane and brave breed of
people called sailors. And a special thanks to
Robert Gilbert, Mike Antoine, and to Mack
& the G Dock Gang, for showing me the true
meaning of "Dramamine."
A salute to you all!!!

Gary Patterson

CONTENTS

PART I

THE
PASSIONATE
SAILOR

1
PASSIONATE SAILING: THE HISTORICAL PRECEDENT

The Passionate Sailor of the twentieth century lives in a diminished world. Gone are the days when sailors like Eric the Red and Blackbeard the Pirate discovered continents, subdued nations, and otherwise ruled the roost. Now *those* were sailors with passion!

But all has not been lost. Even in an age of stinkpots and jet skis, the Passionate Sailor keeps this ancient spirit alive. Whether he's hiking his buns off in a dinghy race, wave-jumping a Windsurfer, or cruising his forty-foot sloop, he's doing it with the same gusto and determination that got the Vikings to Greenland and Captain Bligh kicked off the *Bounty*.

Others may insist that sailing is nothing more than recreation, but for the truly Passionate Sailor sailing is not an escape from reality—it is the *only* reality.

2
THE
PASSIONATE SAILOR
AND HIS BOAT

A Passionate Sailor is most passionate about his boat. While friends and spouses fall by the wayside, he lavishes his craft with every possible gadget and doo-dad, even providing his beloved boat with a Christmas stocking and birthday party—much to the chagrin of his neglected children.

When not in the marine hardware store, the Passionate Sailor is most likely to be found on his boat, coaxing her curvaceous hull and white-bellied sails for every ecstatic knot of performance.

Woe to the one who interferes with the progress of his vessel. If a crewmember lets so much as a finger dip into the water, he'll get a paddle to the knuckles; if a careless stinkpotter so much as nudges her delicate gunwales, he's likely to get that same paddle to the back of the head. The Passionate Sailor is a jealous lover.

GIFTS

3

THE HELM

The Passionate Sailor *always* steers his boat. Other sailors may delight in trimming sails and scrutinizing charts, but not the Passionate Sailor. He is content only when he has his destiny quite literally in his hands. At the tiller or wheel he is master of all that he surveys: the waves breaking at the bow, the sails fluttering in the breeze, and the blue-lipped crew trembling on the weather rail.

The Passionate Sailor is no dummy. He knows that the farther aft you sit, the less likely you are to get wet.

THE ULTIMATE REALITY

4

THE ART OF
CREW MANAGEMENT

He may be without continents to discover and nations to subdue, but the Passionate Sailor still has the essentials: wind, water, a sailboat, and, most important, a crew to abuse. These poor, often unsuspecting individuals pay the price of the Passionate Sailor's all-out pursuit of sport, so it's not surprising that they occasionally show some signs of discontent. Sails suddenly slipping down masts, anchors unexpectedly falling overboard, and winch handles hurled aft are just a few indications that the natives may be getting restless.

The Passionate Sailor has found that intimidation is the best way to keep his crew in line. By subtly altering the timing of otherwise traditional commands, he has discovered a surefire way of turning a potentially rebellious crew into a groveling heap of humanity.

"Ready about"—If said just *after* the boat has swung into the wind, this results in immediate dumping of crew in the water. ("Man overboard" often follows this command but is likely to be inaudible over the crew's screams and the skipper's laughter.)

"Prepare to gybe"—Skipper readies crew for maneuver by commenting that a Man of War jellyfish has just washed up onto the deck. Once crew jumps to feet, command is given, but then only softly and indistinctly; usually results in bruised heads or decapitation.

"Land ho"—Skipper initiates maneuver by calling a crew meeting just aft of mast. Once meeting is under way and contact with rock or shoreline is imminent, command is delivered.

Damage done to the boat and crew during these three maneuvers is usually more than offset by an almost immediate improvement in the crew's attitude. As the weightlifters say, "No pain, no gain!"

5

THE ART OF BACKSEAT SKIPPERING

One of the most difficult times for a Passionate Sailor is when he must watch a less proficient skipper attempt to steer. This usually occurs when a friend or business associate invites him along for a sail. Fortunately, the Passionate Sailor has developed an extremely effective technique for dealing with just this sort of situation.

Before the voyage even begins, he positions himself directly behind the skipper, with his mouth less than two inches from the victim's ear. Once under way, he launches into a commentary intimidating enough to rattle the likes of Ted Turner: "Do you usually sail with the jib luffing like that? I'd suggest you try heading off a few degrees . . . Oops, not so much! Uh-oh, here comes a wave—do you think you can steer around it? No, not like that . . . oh, well—maybe there's a lobster pot wrapped around the rudder. . . "

Usually it isn't long before the victim angrily offers the helm to the Passionate Sailor, who good-naturedly suggests that the erstwhile skipper apply his talents to a less demanding pursuit—such as basketweaving.

6

DEMON RUM

As we all know, the Passionate Sailor has a great deal of respect for those ancient sailing heroes who, with their bellies full of grog, would casually set sail into the teeth of a howling gale or the midst of a blood-thirsty fleet of enemy ships. The Passionate Sailor tries to emulate this booze-induced sangfroid through an intensive and disciplined practice regime. Some might call it a weeklong binge, but for the Passionate Sailor it is just another part of becoming the best he can possibly be.

Day 1: Consume six shots of rum; practice walking down dock. Each time you fall into water, consume another shot. Continue until (a) you have mastered maneuver, (b) nonambulatory inebriety results. (If *b* occurs, wait a day and repeat exercise.)

Day 2: Up initial intake to seven shots; practice getting into dinghy and rowing it to moored boat. If you make it that far, practice stepping from dinghy into boat.

Day 3: Up initial intake to eight shots; practice setting sails. If speech is slurred when shouting orders, splash salt water on face; if face becomes salt-encrusted, switch to tonic water.

Day 4: Up initial intake to nine shots; practice leaving mooring and steering through crowded harbor. If you begin to see double, always aim for leeward-most image; practice until you make it out of harbor.

Day 5: Up initial intake to ten shots; practice sailing upwind. If even slurred speech becomes difficult, develop system of grunts for communicating with crew.

Day 6: Up initial intake to eleven shots; practice sailing downwind. Remember to duck before gybes; take an extra shot each time you don't—you'll need it.

Day 7: Up initial intake to twelve shots; practice docking maneuvers. If seeing double, aim for windward-most image. Once successfully secured to dock, begin mainlining black coffee.

This is a good exercise to repeat at the start of each season. Like anything else, the more you practice it, the better you'll get.

DEMON RUM

7
THE PASSIONATE VS. THE PASSIONLESS SAILOR

It goes without saying that the Passionate Sailors are *not* traditional yachtsmen. Those bluebloods stuck-up enough to call their sailboat a "yacht" are, by definition, almost totally devoid of passion. For them, sailing's chief attraction is that it doesn't require them to sweat.

A yachtsman's attire reflects his staid, stuffy lifestyle, while the Passionate Sailor is not afraid to wear his passion on his sleeve—or anywhere else, for that matter. Given cause (especially the chance to beat the faded red pants off a lockjawed yachtie), the Passionate Sailor is more than willing to let out all the stops—donning duds more suitable for an NFL lineman than a traditional yachtsman.

OLD-SALT PREP

Ancient captain's hat (worn by ancestor on
    Mayflower)
Blue blazer
Brick-red pants
Lacoste shirt with alligator removed
Topsiders
No socks
No life jacket
Pocket watch with gold chain
Tanqueray martini—stirred, never shaken

SAILOR WARRIOR

Visor-equipped hockey helmet
Designer wet or dry suit—take your pick
Sailing gloves equipped with stickum
    fingertips
Bullet-proof life jacket
Iridescent sailing boots with suction soles
Tinted ski goggles
Digital chronometer that also forecasts
    weather
Steroid-laced Gatoraid in squirt bottle

8

PASSIONATE TURN-ONS

A Passionate Sailor's love for the sport isn't exactly platonic. In fact his desire to sail is just that—a burning-hot desire. Here are but a few of his erogenous zones and gear fetishes:

Spinnaker—This bodacious piece of nylon intimidates many lesser sailors, but for the Passionate Sailor its bulging power is part of its appeal. Especially loves to pole it out on a tight reach.

Mylar jib—Headsail made out of new diaphanous, high-tech sailcloth; has the look of a peekaboo, see-through negligee. Loves to watch it luff.

Centerboard—Likes to pull this well-sanded foil up and down its trunk; the tighter the fit, the more sensual.

SPINNAKER

Ball-bearing traveler—Whir of its nylon ball bearings arouses him to trim sails constantly and feverishly.

Ratchet block—Gives him macho sense of power when sheeting in sails; the growlier, the better.

Self-tailing winch—Also instills sense of strength and mastery. Loves to wrap and unwrap lines around its burnished metal sides.

Self-bailer—Automatically sucks water from the bilge; the more noise it makes, the better.

Tiller extension—Best if mounted on a universal joint so he can hold it while in every possible position.

Wind indicator—Yarn or magnetic tape attached to sails and shrouds. Thrills him to watch it dance delicately in the breeze.

9

PASSIONATE BUMMERS

The Passionate Sailor's love (lust) for his sport inevitably coexists with some passionate hates. Here are a few of those occasional blips on that otherwise smooth curve climbing toward ecstasy:

FISHERMEN

For the Passionate Sailor steaming along under spinnaker, no form of *coitus interruptus* is crueler than discovering that a lure is wrapped around his keel and that an aluminum skiff full of beer-swilling hicks is in hot pursuit. Fishermen never seem to give much credence to the Passionate Sailor's claim that, according to Appeal Number 669 of the International Yacht Racing Rules, lures must give sailboats the right-of-way.

BOSUN'S CHAIRS

The Passionate Sailor is most at ease at sea level, but sometimes his services are required at the tippy top of the mast. To get there he must entrust his life and his reproductive organs to a menacing device known as a *bosun's chair*. Once winched slowly and painfully aloft, he attempts to fix something that is almost always unfixable, especially after dropping his screwdriver in the distant drink.

FISHERMAN

ENGINES

A Passionate Sailor would much rather do
without an engine, but if his boat is over
twenty-five feet long, it is one of those
unavoidable realities of the twentieth century.
Since he uses his engine only when absolutely
necessary, he never becomes very good at
operating it (he always seems to confuse
forward and reverse as well as fast and slow),
and many are the docks he's permanently
defaced with his bow. It's little wonder then
that whenever the Passionate Sailor keys on
the "Iron Staysail" his crew immediately runs
screaming into the cabin.

FOG

The wind dies to nothing, the sun disappears,
and suddenly the salt won't come out of the
shaker. Fog socks in only when the compass
and depth sounder are on the blink.

SOCKED IN

SEASICKNESS

Amusement parks may make money delivering this sensation to millions of kids each year, but the Passionate Sailor no longer gets a thrill out of hanging his head over the leeward rail and puking his guts out. However, he does derive a certain sense of satisfaction when *others* are so afflicted, often taking the opportunity to offer them a moldy baloney and liverwurst sandwich he saves just for such occasions.

(TALKING) HEADS

No one is quite sure how marine toilets are supposed to work, mainly because they usually don't. The only thing a head is guaranteed to do is make a series of rude, verging-on-obscene gurgles, groans, and grunts that the rest of the crew inevitably assumes is being caused by the person wrestling with this odious contraption. As far as the Passionate Sailor is concerned, it is a needless distraction from the job at hand. So if nature calls when you're on board his boat, don't be surprised when he hands you a three-dollar plastic bucket with the instructions to empty it to leeward.

THE INITIATION

CLEANING THE BOTTOM

If he could keelhaul Mr. Clean, this wouldn't be so bad, but such is not the case. For the Passionate Sailor, bristle-brushing slime while treading water in a polluted harbor is right up there with cleaning urinals in a New York City subway station.

LAUNCH DRIVERS

After a long, wonderful day of sailing, nothing rankles the Passionate Sailor more than a long, frustrating wait for a ride back to the dock. Launch drivers tend to be college kids on the make, so unless the Passionate Sailor looks terrific in a bikini, the chances of getting picked up before midnight are next to nil.

SPRING CLEANING

10

THE SAILING INSTRUCTOR

Unlike their more traditional, blueblood counterparts, Passionate Sailors aren't born with tillers in their hands. This means that they must learn how to sail the hard way—by submitting to that most humiliating of indignities: a Sailing School.

Few things in life can match the degradation of being tormented by a punk-kid sailing instructor whose idea of fun is watching a middle-aged landlubber make a fool of himself in a sailboat. The sailing instructor uses his knowledge of arcane phrases like *bow* and *stern* to bewilder the beginner until he falls helplessly to the cockpit floor.

This experience completely turns many people off to the sport. But for the individual who is destined to become a Passionate Sailor, it is what fuels his determination to excel at this thing called y*aa*hting. As he lies there cheek-to-jowl with the bilge, the Passionate-Sailor-to-be makes a solemn vow: "Someday I'm gonna blow this kid outta the water, someday...."

THE INSTRUCTOR

11

THE DINGHY RACE

To the uninitiated, a sailboat race is about as breathtaking as watching grapes shrivel into raisins. However, all it takes is one ride on a Passionate Sailor's boat to appreciate the subtlety and excitement of this fascinating form of competition.

THE START

A ten-minute ritual resembling the mating dance of an oversexed school of killer whales precedes the race as sailors jockey for position on an imaginary line between the race-committee boat and buoy. The Passionate Sailor spends most of this time planted squarely on the line, intimidating nearby boats with a continual stream of verbal abuse. Seconds prior to the start the officials in the committee boat turn their backs to the fleet, fire the starting gun, and shout "ALL CLEAR!" The race is on.

THE FIRST BEAT

The fleet crosses the line on starboard tack, although there are some notable exceptions that quickly get skewered by the bows of onrushing boats. The Passionate Sailor frantically wiggles the tiller and rocks his torso, but what at first seems to be the latest brand of "body kinetics" is actually caused by a bee that has somehow gotten into the pants of his foul-weather gear. While he screams at his crew to rip off his clothes, the other boats begin to tack on wind shifts.

MARK ROUNDING

THE MARK ROUNDING

As they approach the first mark, boats that have dispersed in every imaginable direction suddenly converge into one great howling mass of splintering fiberglass and ripping sails. The resultant chaos allows the Passionate Sailor to gain back all that he has lost; in fact, by steering around the boats locked in hand-to-hand combat in the vicinity of the buoy, he quickly catapults himself into first place.

THE RUN

Since he is now sailing with the wind, the Passionate Sailor quickly raises his spinnaker, as do the boats directly behind him. Now the tension becomes almost unbearable on board our hero's boat as the fleet behind leaves him hardly enough air to breathe, let alone fill his sails. His competitors inch closer and closer while the Passionate Sailor and his crew gasp for breath. Never has the term *choking* had a more appropriate application.

YET ANOTHER MARK ROUNDING

Miraculously, the Passionate Sailor gets around the last buoy just before the entire fleet stampedes over him. Now that he's on the final sprint to the finish, it's time to consolidate his position at the front of the pack by "covering" his nearest competitor. This proves to be none other than Fenton Fosdick III—the person who years ago taught our hero how to sail (see Chapter 10, "The Sailing Instructor"). There is no one on this earth he would rather pummel to a pulp.

THE LAST BEAT

Our hero and Fosdick become embroiled in a bitter "tacking duel" to the finish, involving no less than 219 tacks and twice as many expletives. The Passionate Sailor's expertise is the expletives; Fosdick's is the tacking. Going into the finish, it looks like Fosdick is about to pass our hero. Just when the situation looks hopeless, the Passionate Sailor seizes the spinnaker pole, hurls it valiantly at the rival skipper, and knocks him into the water. Fosdick's boat capsizes as our hero crosses the line victorious!

Unfortunately, once Fosdick's boat is righted, his crew hoists a red "protest" flag, accusing the Passionate Sailor of breaking the rules of yacht racing as well as human decency in general. A protest meeting is scheduled for later that evening at the yacht club.

THE PROTEST MEETING

The Passionate Sailor enters the protest meeting dressed in judicial robes. In his hand are a copy of the yacht racing rules and a Bible. Fosdick appears in a wheelchair with his head wrapped in a bandage. During the meeting our hero lies passionately and shamelessly, but it is not enough. The judges see it Fosdick's way and throw the Passionate Sailor out of the race.

THE BAR

Now comes the final postrace catharsis. Using empty rum bottles as boats, the Passionate Sailor and his crew endlessly rehash the race. Not surprisingly, the strength of their performance increases with each retelling, as does the injustice of the judges' decision. By the end of the evening they are enthusiastic for revenge. Even in defeat, there is always another race.

PROTEST MEETING

12

THE FAMILY CRUISE

The Passionate Sailor's wife has been hounding him for the last two years to take her and the kids for a cruise. "All you do is sail," she quite rightly points out. "Why can't you include us?" Finally, with great reluctance, he makes arrangements for a weekend cruise with their three children and Labrador retriever on a friend's thirty-foot sloop.

THE DEPARTURE

They are motoring out of the harbor on a fine summer morning when the dog decides to relieve himself on the foredeck. The Passionate Sailor hands the helm over to his wife, then goes forward to clean up the mess. As he swabs down the deck, he is knocked inexplicably to his knees. His wife (while trying to settle a dispute between their two sons) has steered them into a channel marker—doing no damage to the buoy but putting a $500 gash in the borrowed boat's bow.

A TEST OF SEAMANSHIP

After inspecting the hole, he decides to continue with the cruise but immediately regrets his decision when he discovers that his four-year-old daughter has flushed a chart down the head, rendering it useless. However, once the sails are set and they are reaching along nicely under the big number one gennie, he begins to feel better.

It's about then that a line of storm clouds suddenly appears on the horizon. Before he has a chance to shorten sail, they are caught in forty knots of driving rain. The children cower in the cabin while his wife screams, "Make the boat stop tipping!" To accomplish this, he single-handedly reefs the main and changes to a smaller jib; his wife clings white-knuckled to the tiller and prays.

TEST OF SEAMANSHIP

THE ANCHORAGE

Finally the storm passes, and they arrive at a quaint and peaceful harbor. Unfortunately, all the slips at the marina are taken. The Passionate Sailor decides they'll anchor in a nearby cove.

It turns out to be a beautiful spot, and his wife has begun to gush poetically about the raptures of sail when his twelve-year-old son throws out the anchor but forgets to secure the line to the boat. Two hours later, on his 99th dive underwater, the Passionate Sailor locates the anchor in the mud.

THE V-BERTH EPIPHANY

By this time he is blue with cold and wants desperately to sleep. After eating cold Spaghetti-Os out of the can (no one can get the alcohol stove to work), the family finally beds down for the night. He and his wife share the V-berth with their squirming daughter while their two boys have already begun to snore in the aft cabin.

As exhaustion drags him steadily toward sleep, an unlikely smile begins to flicker on his face. The Passionate Sailor is amazed to discover that, even though everything went wrong, it wasn't *that* bad a day after all. In fact, this cruising stuff is kind of fun!

THE ANCHORAGE

13

RULES OF THUMB

For years sailors have kept a sea locker's worth of tried-and-true nautical jingles that help them remember such basic things as:

> Red sky at night,
> Sailor's delight.

Well, the Passionate Sailors of the twentieth century have updated these traditional apothegms to keep them in touch with the modern-day realities of the sport. Here are but a few:

> Jet ski ahead,
> Sailor sees red.

> Keel in the air,
> Sailor beware.

> Mast in the mud,
> Pray for a flood.

KEEL IN THE AIR

Bird dung in beer,
Seagull is near.

Bilge water blue,
Lot of bailing to do.
Bilge water brown,
Head must be down.

Burning legs, peeling nose,
Too much sun, too few clothes.

DUNG IN BEER

Square knot, double hitch,
Sheep shank too,
All these knots—
But whatta they do?

Booze in the icebox,
Wind in my sails,
See ya later, docks,
Hello, happy trails!

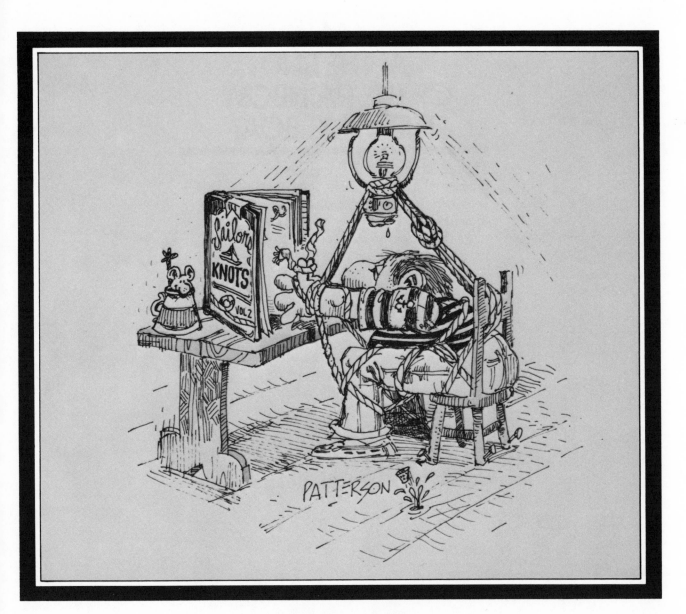

SQUARE KNOT

14
AT THE END
OF THE RAINBOW:
THE MAXI-BOAT

The secret dream of all Passionate Sailors—no matter what kind of boat they currently sail—is to own that most glorious of behemoths: a Maxi-Boat.

As the name suggests, there is nothing bigger on the racecourses across the globe. Almost a hundred feet in length, one of these grand gorgeous Goliaths requires a football team's worth of crew and a budget the size of the Pentagon's.

If the Passionate Sailor owned a maxi, he would have no need for a house, a car, or anything else for that matter. And maybe, just maybe, he would admit that he had finally become a yachtsman—a Passionate Yachtsman, of course.

15
ARE YOU A PASSIONATE SAILOR? THE TRUE TEST

If you are a Passionate Sailor, you'll find the following quiz pretty straightforward.

1. If a smaller sailboat costing thousands of dollars less than yours passes you, do you:
   a. **wave to the other skipper and compliment him on his boat's performance?**
   b. **stomp up and down, bite the tiller in half, then scream at your crew to change to a larger headsail?**

2. If your crew puts up the spinnaker sideways, do you:
   a. **patiently explain what they did wrong and ask them to try it again?**
   b. **begin pelting them with turnbuckles, beer cans, and any other objects close at hand?**

3. If a thundercloud appears on the horizon, do you:
   a. **immediately reduce sail and head for the nearest port?**
   b. **begin humming the theme from *Rocky* while altering course in the thunderhead's direction?**

STORM WARNING

4. When you enter a marine hardware store, do you:
   a. **locate the item you want, pay for it, and leave?**
   b. **begin to run around the place, compulsively collecting every piece of equipment you might someday need?**

5. When a crew member complains that he or she is wet, cold, or otherwise uncomfortable, do you:
   a. **listen sympathetically, then try to relieve the person's discomfort?**
   b. **shrug your shoulders and snarl, "WIMP"?**

6. If a boat near you makes an unsuccessful attempt at picking up a mooring, do you:
   a. **pretend not to have noticed?**
   b. **break into derisive laughter?**

7. If another boat mistakenly crashes into yours, do you:
   a. **immediately ask if everybody is OK?**
   b. **jump into the cockpit of the other boat and start to strangle its skipper?**

BUMP ATTACK

8. If you happen to run aground, do you:
   a. **apologize to your crew for sailing too close to shore?**
   b. **attribute the accident to unnaturally low tides caused by Halley's comet?**

9. When sailing in a flat calm, do you:
   a. **sit back, relax, and work on your tan?**
   b. **hoist your youngest child to the top of the mast and tell him to look for wind?**

10. When at a party given by nonsailors, do you:
    a. **talk wittily about literature, art, and current events?**
    b. **resort to floating paper boats in the punch bowl?**

BEACHED

PART II
PASSIONATE TYPES

16

THE DIVERSITY OF SAIL

Unlike most sports in which everybody does basically the same thing (e.g., all bowlers roll the same big black ball; all golfers hit the same little white ball), there are as many ways to sail as there are sailboats. For example, someone who bobs around a minuscule lake in a Styrofoam "Kool" boat has little in common with a multihull sailor who has just slammed into a whale on his way across the Atlantic Ocean.

What follows is a representative sampling of the many different types of sailors. To apply some method to the madness, they've been grouped into three equally passionate categories: Racers, Cruisers, and Off-the-Beachers.

THAT CERTAIN FEELING

17

RACERS

Like snowflakes, no two Passionate Racers are the same, although they all have one thing in common: an insatiable craving for silverware. They want to win, and they want to win badly—no matter what the cost.

A racer's need to succeed is directly proportional to the size of his ego, which in most cases can only be described as humongous. Yes, a Passionate Racer tends to be a fairly confident individual, strutting down the dock with all the humility of David Lee Roth at a Girl Scouts convention—especially when he's got yet another trophy glittering in his hands.

THE RACER

THE CLUB CHAMP

Way back when, he attended a national
championship in a far-off state, and the
T-shirt they gave him hasn't been off his back
since. He still refers to all the famous sailors
he competed against by their first names, even
though the closest he ever got to them was at
the registration desk before the regatta
began.

Ever since his trip to the big leagues, he's
regarded the racing at his home club as
hopelessly trivial. As far as he's concerned,
he's doing his local fleet a favor by simply
giving them a peek at his championship
T-shirt (which is developing some unsettling
holes).

One of these days, the Club Champ insists,
he's going to go back to the nationals to
experience some more *real* competition (as
well as pick up a new shirt). Until that time,
he likes to think of himself as the biggest,
baddest fish in an itsy-bitsy pond.

THE HUSBAND AND WIFE TEAM

They have delayed having children because they are having so much fun competing in their two-person Olympic-class dinghy. But you have to wonder. A trip around the buoys with this couple is like following a waterborne version of divorce court. Every maneuver, it seems, is proceeded by a violent argument, if not downright fisticuffs.

Husband: "OK, let's tack and go over to the left side of the course."

Wife: "You're nuts. The right side is favored."

Husband: "Whaddayamean? Look at the boats in that corner!"

Wife: "I tell you, the wind is going to shift, it's going to—"

Husband: "Why are you giving me such a hard time?"

Wife: "*Me* giving *you* a hard time? Why every time I—"

Husband: "Honey, put that spinnaker pole down, please put that—"

Wife: "So, are we going to stay on this tack and go to the right side?"

Husband: "Well, ahem, maybe you're right; maybe the wind will shift after all . . . "

Wife: "I love it when we work as a team."

THE SINGLE-HANDER

When he's racing a sailboat, he likes to do it all and he likes to do it alone, but most of all he likes to hike. His toes locked under abrasive "hiking" straps, his posterior hanging out over the angular, thigh-incising edge of the boat, and his torso hunched beneath a truckload of soggy, mildewed sweatshirts, he grunts and grimaces his way over every wave.

The Single-Hander loves pain; he's even built a device known as a "hiking bench" so that he can indulge in this peculiar form of masochism in the privacy of his own basement. It's enough to make the Marquis de Sade jealous.

The Single-Hander may do it alone, but, oh (ow!) does he do it!

HIKING OUT

THE FROSTBITER

This is the lunatic fringe of the lunatic fringe: a person who races sailboats in subfreezing temperatures and claims he enjoys it.

A true Frostbiter sails *only* in the winter. For him, sailing isn't sailing unless ice cubes are floating in the bilge and icicles are hanging from the boom. He also likes being bundled up in so many layers that he has the dimensions of the Pillsbury Doughboy. But what *really* turns the Frostbiter on is the prospect of a cold-water capsize: the bite of frigid water and the panicky shock of being unable to breathe, but most of all, the chance to call it quits ahead of time.

For the Frostbiter, the real joy is not the sailing, but the recuperation period in the yacht club bar—especially when the rest of those crazies are still out there freezing off their derrières!

THE FROSTBITER

THE DAYSAILOR

His boat looks more like Noah's Ark than a modern sailboat, sporting a huge cuddy and cockpit, a micro sailplan, and an ice chest the size of a walk-in freezer. However, the Daysailor is a wolf in sheep's clothing.

He may *appear* to be in no hurry as he sails casually down the bay—beer in one hand, tiller in the other—but he has the heart and soul of the most fiendish sort of racer. Nothing gives the Daysailor more pleasure than passing another sailboat.

The trick is to do it while looking as if he couldn't care less. To accomplish this, he and his crew have developed a system of code words to hide the fact that they're actually giving it all they've got:

"Hand me another frostie."
Translation: "Trim the jib."
"See that fish jumpin' yonder?"
Translation: "Ease the main."
"I think I'm gonna catch a few Zs."
Translation: "Set the spinnaker." (This purposely tattered sail, like everything else on his boat, looks a lot slower than it really is.)

Once the Daysailor (whose boat is called *Bessie*) passes his shocked and humiliated prey, he crowns his achievement by gazing over the transom and commenting, "Well look at this. We've been draggin' an umbrella, and it's open!"

74

THE ROCK STAR

In the lingo of sailing, the term *rock star* doesn't refer to a teen idol with an electric guitar strapped to his groin but to an even stranger form of life—a person who is paid (under the table, of course) to race sailboats.

A while back, the Rock Star made a name for himself by winning sailing's Holy Grail: the America's Cup. Ever since, however, his career has been a series of near and not-so-near misses. To compensate for his lack of success on the racecourse, the Rock Star has become a master of the media game. He's hired a press agent to ensure plenty of good publicity and a makeup team to tend to his Marlboro Man good looks. (It's rumored that his aviator sunglasses have been surgically affixed to prevent unsightly slippage.)

Although he is a visible part of almost every big-time sailing event, it is still the America's Cup that provides his most productive time in the limelight. Even while losing miserably, the Rock Star manages to steal the headlines by publicly questioning his opponents' sexual preferences.

The Rock Star knows all too well that it's behind a microphone—not a wheel—that he's happiest. If sailing had a broadcast booth, he would be in it.

THE OWNER

The Owner of a big racing boat on the Grand Prix circuit is, by definition, rich. However, he is not necessarily much of a sailor. He's in it purely for the prestige and glory, preferring to sit back in the cockpit and watch his hired guns dance around his brand-new, hi-tech rocketship.

He runs his boat like a business—a business he doesn't know much about. If his boat doesn't win, he simply fires the entire crew and hires a new one. Unfortunately, now that he's on his thirteenth boat and forty-fifth crew, he's finding qualified and willing sailors harder and harder to find.

But this doesn't bother the Owner. As long as he has the bucks, he's confident that he'll eventually be able to buy his way to the top. And he's probably right.

THE OWNER

18

CRUISERS

As far as racers are concerned, those who cruise are those who lose. If they were *real* sailors, the racers maintain, they would be willing to put their skills to the test on the starting line.

Of course, the Passionate Cruisers of the world see it quite differently. As far as they're concerned, sailors who beat their brains out on a rinky-dink racecourse are no better than those hyperactive hamsters you see spinning their wheels in a pet shop.

According to the Cruiser, the challenges of passagemaking are much more in keeping with the glorious tradition of sail. Can you imagine a clipper ship captain submitting himself to the indignity of a protest meeting? No, the Cruiser insists, *he* best epitomizes the truly Passionate Sailor.

THE GUNKHOLER

Impossible-to-find inlets, inaccessible coves, and out-of-the-way harbors are the domain of the Gunkholer. In fact he has a phobia for the wide-open bays and sounds in which most of us like to sail.

The Gunkholer's idea of a good time is "exploring" places where other sailors fear to tread, even braving low-hanging branches and rocky shoals in his search for a secluded nook to throw out the hook. As a consequence, the tip of his mast looks like a half-eaten pretzel, while his keel resembles a barnacled piece of scrap metal.

The Gunkholer likes to think of himself as a modern-day Columbus, but in truth his obsession with shore-hugging stems from a rather unromantic fact: The Gunkholer can't swim!

THE NAVIGATOR

If he's going any distance at all, the Passionate Cruiser can't do without an equally passionate Navigator—a man who always knows where he is going. He's the only one on the boat with clip-on sunglasses, and he keeps a calculator strapped to his belt. To be brutally honest, he is a nerd.

His below-decks station is crammed with every kind of high-tech navigational device known to mankind—Loran, Weatherfax, Caltron, Pac Man . . . you name it, and the Navigator can boot it up on his video screen. He can provide in an instant the speed of the boat, its present longitude and latitude, wind direction, water depth, and the precise location of the nearest lobster pot, as well as the number of lobsters it contains.

Since he already knows where he's headed, the Navigator has no desire to actually see what's drifting by the boat. So he remains gleefully glued to his nav station, leaving his less cerebral crewmembers to enjoy all those mundane things like sun, wind, and water.

THE NAVIGATOR

THE BOAT BUM

His stubble enables him to sand the bottom of the boat with his face, and he still wears the same Grateful Dead T-shirt he wore to his college graduation many moons ago. Unwilling to abandon his sixties ideals for a "real" job, the Boat Bum has made a life of delivering large sailboats all across the world, while dabbling in a wee bit of drug trafficking just to make ends meet.

He is most comfortable sleeping on a wet sailbag in an exotic port and can drink almost anyone under the table—something he finds himself doing with increasing frequency. The Boat Bum has seen it all through the salt-spattered lenses of his sunglasses, and someday he plans to make some sense of it. Until that day, he'll hang out his thumb in search of yet another voyage to yet another distant and beckoning paradise.

THE BOAT BUM

THE CHARTERBOATER

Every winter thousands of cabin-feverish sailors migrate to the Caribbean, where they indulge in the weeklong ritual of the Charterboat Cruise. This is sailing's answer to Club Med—a process in which the delights of sun- and alcohol-poisoning obliterate all memories of the cold cruel world to the north.

In preparation for the trip, the Charterboater packs seven brand-new bathing suits (and nothing else) while making arrangements to have a Jamaican bartender on duty in the boat's galley. Since the Caribbean winds never change and the shorelines are all sand, the sailing is virtually idiot-proof, which is a good thing considering the capabilities (or lack thereof) of the Charterboater and his crew.

Midway through the week they are ablaze with second-degree burns, but no matter— they are feeling no pain . . . at least until the plane trip home.

CHARTERBOAT

THE GLOBE-TROTTER

Every ten years or so, the Globe-Trotter decides to sell his house, quit his job, and cruise the Seven Seas until his money runs out. If he has a family, he drags them along with him; if he doesn't, he advertises for a young, blonde female interested in nonstop sailing and sex but must ultimately go it alone when the only woman to answer his ad weighs more than his keel.

Money is tight during his cruise, so the Globe-Trotter tries to sell his story to every available sailing magazine. Since the cruising life is almost always dreadfully dull, he seeks out all available hurricanes, monsoons, tidal waves, gales, etc. The sailing is harrowing, but at least it generates good copy.

Finally, when he is down to his last penny, he purposely sinks his vessel in the mid-Atlantic. The tale of his two months in a raft provides him with a spot on "Good Morning America," a lecture tour, and the money needed to buy a new and bigger boat; there's even a blonde interested in accompanying him on his next cruise.

Not even Blackbeard had it this good!

THE GLOBE-TROTTER

THE WOODENBOATER

In the sixties the Woodenboater lived in a commune; in the seventies he lived in a condominium; in the Eighties he reassessed his values, moved to Maine, and now lives on his all-natural boat. The Woodenboater dresses in hiking boots, flannel shirts, and suspenders and would much rather inhale wood dust and paint fumes than feel the splash of salt spray on his face.

What interests this bearded worshiper of nautical nostalgia is the care and feeding of his no-artificial-anything boat. The hull is wood, the sails are Egyptian cotton, and the lines are hemp. Although beautiful and quaint, these materials require countless hours of maintenance, which he quite proudly refers to as "restoration." Yes, the Woodenboater is happiest when varnishing the brightwork, humming old sea chanteys, and staying tethered most securely to the dock.

THE WOODENBOATER

19

OFF-THE-BEACHERS

These are the bad boys and girls of sailing—brash blonde beer drinkers who belong to no yacht club and are proud of it. Instead, they frequent the beach where the sailing is cheap and the conditions are breezy.

To add insult to injury, they don't sail traditional sit-on-your-duff sailboats, preferring to dash over the waves on outlandish craft that weren't even invented a few short decades ago.

Off-the-Beachers are not an elitist crowd, and anyone is welcome. However, if you happen to be over thirty, have a less-than-lovely bod, or don't enjoy shouting "Aw Right!" every ten seconds, you may feel a little bit out of place.

THE BOARDSAILOR

The traditionalists maintain that what the Boardsailor does isn't really sailing at all, but a form of degeneracy akin to drugs, sex, and rock 'n' roll. In truth, the Boardsailor does have too much fun for his own good: a wishbone in his hands and a wave-washed surfboard at his feet, he blasts along at speeds that make even an America's Cup skipper jealous.

Boardsailing is also a lot harder than it looks. Many are the yachtsmen who have thrown out their backs and otherwise bruised their egos while attempting to show just how easy this beach-toy stuff really is.

To top it all off, boardsailing is fun to watch—and so are its devotees. Colorful and scanty swimsuits are the norm, but when the goosebumps start to interfere with the tan, a wet suit—preferably hot pink—will do just fine, as long as it matches the color scheme of the sail.

THE CAT SAILOR

As far as the cat sailor is concerned, what's already pretty good with one hull is twice as good with two. His boat is fast—faster than anything on the water that doesn't eat gasoline—enabling him to motor past those frumpy monohulls as if they were standing still. The cat sailor also has a trampoline to bounce around on between those two knifelike hulls, as well as dual trapezes on which he and his crew hang out over the water like a pair of wave-skimming Wallendas.

But the cat sailor must pay a price for his glamorous and glorious place in the sun. The faster his double-barreled hot rod goes, the more likely it is to "pitchpole"—the moral equivalent of slamming into a retaining wall. First the bows dig in, then the cat somersaults head over heels, whipping the crew around on their trapeze wires before dumping them most ignominiously into the water.

Putting the pedal to the metal on a catamaran may be risky, but it's what makes life in the fast lane so much fun.

ABANDON SHIP

20

PASSIONATE SAILING: THE ULTIMATE REALITY

All Passionate Sailors, whether they be Racers, Cruisers, or Off-the-Beachers, share a common belief: the game of sailing is no game. Its joys and sorrows are as real as, if not *more* real than, life itself.

And so, as our Passionate Sailor steers bravely into the sunset, he leaves us with one final, heart-felt epigram:

You've got to keep on bailing,
Sharpen that rigging knife,
'Cause life is sailing
And sailing is life.

SAILING IS LIFE